African Magic Series

VOODOO OF LOUISIANA

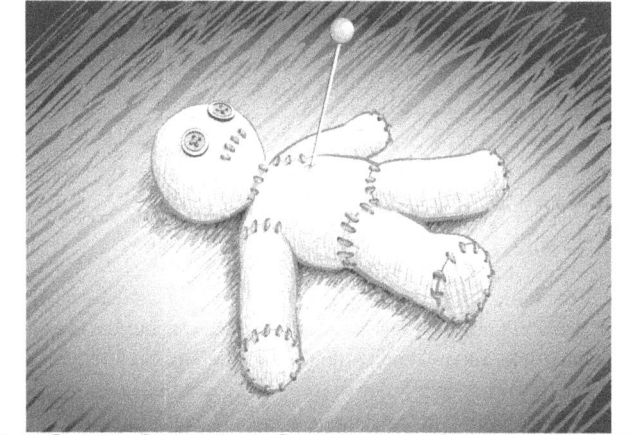

MONIQUE JOINER SIEDLAK

Oshun
Publications

Voodoo of Louisiana © 2019 Monique Joiner Siedlak

All rights reserved. This book or parts thereof may not be reproduced in any form, stored in any retrieval system, or transmitted in any form by any means—electronic, mechanical, photocopy, recording, or otherwise—without prior written permission of the publisher, except as provided by United States of America copyright law.

Under no circumstances will any blame or legal responsibility be held against the publisher, or author, for any damages, reparation, or monetary loss due to the information contained within this book. Either directly or indirectly.

ISBN-13:978-1-948834-95-7

Publisher

Oshun Publications, LLC

Legal Notice:

This book is copyright protected. This book is only for personal use. You cannot amend, distribute, sell, use, quote or paraphrase any part, or the content within this book, without the consent of the author or publisher.

Disclaimer Notice:

Please note the information contained within this document is for educational and entertainment purposes only. All effort has been executed to present accurate, up to date, and reliable, complete information. No warranties of any kind are declared or implied. Readers acknowledge that the author is not engaging in the rendering of legal, financial, medical or professional advice. The content within this book has been derived from various sources. Please consult a licensed professional before attempting any techniques outlined in this book.

By reading this document, the reader agrees that under no circumstances is the author responsible for any losses, direct or indirect, which are incurred as a result of the use of information contained within this document, including, but not limited to, — errors, omissions, or inaccuracies.

Cover Design by MJS

Cover Image by Depositphotos.com

Contents

Other Books in Series	v
A Great Offer	vii
Newsletter Sign Up	ix
1. What is Voodoo?	1
2. The Real History of Voodoo	5
3. Voodoo Post-Haitian Revolution	7
4. Voodoo and Racism	11
5. How Voodoo Influenced Hoodoo	15
6. Myths and Facts of Voodoo	19
7. Voodoo Temples	23
8. The Loas	27
9. The Voodoo Queens	49
10. Voodoo Kings	55
11. Voodoo Practices: What You Need To Know	59
12. Voodoo Symbols	73
Glossary	81
About the Author	85
Other Books by Monique Joiner Siedlak	87
Please Review	89

Other Books in Series

African Spirituality Beliefs and Practices
Hoodoo
Seven African Powers: The Orishas
Cooking for the Orishas
Lucumi: The Ways of Santeria

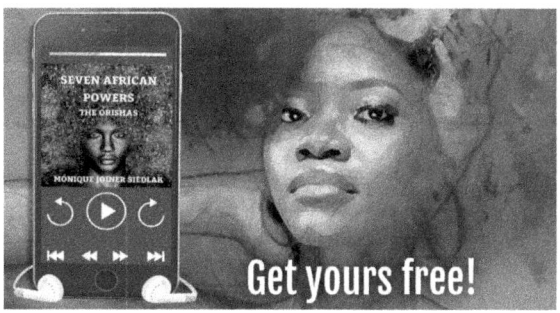

Want to learn about African Magic, Wicca, or even Reiki while cleaning your home, exercising, or driving to work? I know it's tough these days to simply find the time to relax and curl up with a good book. This is why I'm delighted to share that I have books available in audiobook format.

Best of all, you can get the audiobook version of this book or any other book by me for free as part of a 30-day Audible trial.

Members get free audiobooks every month and exclusive discounts. It's an excellent way to explore and determine if audiobook learning works for you.

If you're not satisfied, you can cancel anytime within the trial period. You won't be charged, and you can still keep your book. To choose your free audiobook, visit:

www.mojosiedlak.com/free-audiobooks

WANT UPDATES, FREEBIES & GIVEAWAYS?!

MONIQUE JOINER SIEDLAK

THE ORISHAS

JOIN MY NEWSLETTER!

mojosiedlak.com/newsletter-signup

ONE

What is Voodoo?

Voodoo is something that just about everyone has heard or seen in movies or read about in books. The version of voodoo which is depicted in movies or books is usually with regards to one genre, and that is horror. There is more to voodoo then what one might think which is why it is a good idea to learn more about it.

First, we need to talk about what voodoo isn't to understand what it actually is. It isn't black magic, devil worship or a cult and people who practice it aren't sorcerers, witchdoctors or occultists. Don't think that voodoo is intended for hurting or controlling others as most voodooists haven't even seen what a voodoo doll looks like unless they saw it in a movie.

So Just What is Voodoo?

It is a religion which has origins from Africa. The voodoo religion in the Americas or the Caribbean is actually a combination of different Catholic, African and Native American traditions. The belief is followed by many throughout the world, but there is no proper estimate of Voodooists.

The religion does not have any scripture or a world authority like the Catholic Church. Voodooists focus more on a community-centered experience that supports empowerment, responsibility and individual experience. Voodoo is entirely different across different parts of the globe and even varies from community to community.

Voodoo is all-embracing and takes the entire human experience into account. Its adherents are those who believe that they are imperfect or want to have a religion in line with their own purposes. Voodooists have gone through a strong history due to slavery by the Europeans.

How Did Voodoo Move Around the World?

Despite all we know about voodoo now, the exact origin of this religion and the practices are still unknown.

The word Voodoo or Vodoun or Vodou is said to have a Benin origin meaning a fearsome and mysterious kind of power. This power is said to possess the priest who acts as the mouthpiece between the world of the spirits and the living.

The voodoo religion, cult or belief spread through the word as slave trades on going through the world, voodoo was a way by which these slaves communicated and worshipped in a foreign land.

Many wonder how the Catholic faith got entwined in voodoo, the white master didn't understand the religion and incantations rites performed by the slaves, and to stop them they imposed the Catholic faith upon them. Some of the slaves desist from the voodoo rituals while others just blended the Catholic belief into what they understood and made it new.

So What Do Voodooists Believe In?

To understand what the Voodooists believe in, one has first to know how a Voodooist sees the world around him. Voodooists have a belief that there is an invisible and visible world and that these two worlds have been intertwined together. They all have the impression that one dies, they transition to the hidden world and due to this, and our predecessors are always with us in spirit.

Besides the belief that their ancestors are with them in

spirit, Voodooists also believe in Loa which is described as an archetype of human personalities (for example Ogun the warrior). They think that each Loa is, in reality, a family member of similar types. Voodooists try to develop a relationship with Loa for help in the visible world and for advice. It is quite similar to the secular practice of learning and even honoring famous historical figures such as someone might want to find inspiration from Muhammad Ali Jinnah who fought the British for an independent state (Pakistan) or either Michael Jackson if they're going to make it big in the music industry.

The Loa are seen as accessible and helpers of human beings. Voodoo is just like any other religion with many followers around the world and is a more accepting religion than other major world religions like Islam, Christianity or Judaism.

TWO

The Real History of Voodoo

There is more to the history of voodoo than one might come to believe. Voodooists have different beliefs, but the main article of faith is that of universal energy and the soul which leaves the body during dreams and of spirit possession. Whereas, in Abrahamic belief such as Islam or even Christianity, a spiritual property is thought to be an act of Satan or a demonic entity. Something which is trying to penetrate the human vessel and in Voodoo being possessed by Loa is desired and deemed to be valuable to the person possessed as they believe that the person has a connection with the spirit world.

History of Voodoo

The Voodoo religion originated in the Americas or the Caribbean when the Europeans had brought slaves from West Africa to the New World. These slaves combined different elements of Western African, Native American and even Roman Catholic traditions to form the Voodoo religion which is practiced today around the world. In 1685, the law banned the practice of any African religions, and all slaves were required by their masters to be Christianized within 8 days from their arrival to the Americas.

These African slaves were forcefully converted and even

forced to adopt Catholic rituals which led to the creation of their religion. Many of the spirits of the slaves became associated with Christian saints, and one of these spirits is the Ogun which is the Nigerian spirit of hunting, ironsmiths, and warfare. Thus, Ogun became Ogou which inspired many political revolutions to oust oppressive regimes.

Followers of Voodoo were persecuted by just about everyone including the authorities who regularly demonized the religion. One of the false books published was Hayti or the Black Republic in 1889 and falsely attributed cannibalism, sacrifices and other atrocities with the religion. Even today, many Christians still regard the religion with black magic, Satanism and Occult. The word is used as an adjective to refer to anything mysterious, unknowable or unworkable. The doctrine has faced racism and is still struggling with racism.

Voodoo and Zombies

The idea that Voodoo is associated with the belief in zombies and animal sacrifices has been used by television shows to fantasize the religion as something eerie. The use of zombies is an excellent example of how the religious element of Voodoo has been taken out for use by the media at its own whim.

The belief in zombies is paramount to the religion, and it is said that the original Haitian zombies were not villains but rather victims. It is noted that the Haitian zombies were actually people who had been brought back from the dead. The ritual of turning someone into a zombie was seen as a punishment for any abuse or misconduct. It is even said that zombies had also been used as slave labor to work on sugarcane plantation even though there is no evidence to suggest this.

Faced an Underserved Reputation

Voodoo has met a rather sizeable underserved reputation of being sinister. Even though the Voodoo religion does require some animal sacrifice but so does Islam and other Abrahamic faiths like Christianity and Judaism.

THREE

Voodoo Post-Haitian Revolution

Voodoo has become a sensationalized caricature in pop-culture referring to Vodoun or simply Voodoo which actually is a biased appropriation of the Afro-Caribbean religion which originates from Haiti. The doctrine has followers in Jamaica, United States, Dominican Republic, and Brazil and in many other parts of the world. The religion has been belittled to just voodoo dolls or zombies.

The Voodoo religion consists of various cultural elements. The practices, personal creeds, folk medical practices, and stories are told across generations. Voodoo is more than just a religion but is instead a way of life. The religion teaches a universal belief in the Supreme Being referred to as Bondye, a creator God. The believers of the religious worship various spirits known as Loa and each of these spirits is responsible for a specific part of life. Haiti is the country with one of the largest population of Voodooists and has experienced a lot due to its religion.

Haitian Revolution

Ever since the post-Haitian revolution, Voodoo has changed a lot in the country. It was the greatest war fought by

Africans for their rights and freedom. The religion helped the first slaves wage war against colonial masters for independence. They fought against French rule in the 18th century and were victorious.

It was the Voodoo priestess who supervised the Haitian slaves to come together for the first time and wage war against their colonial masters to be free from oppression. The Haitian Revolution took place in 1791 to 1804 and is the only country where slaves found freedom through force. Haiti was the first Latin American country to gain independence.

It was the Voodoo Ceremony in August of 1791 referred to as liberty which set out the plan for attacking plantations, burning them down and killing all the white planters they came in contact with.

United Under One Religion

Voodoo is what united all the Haitian slaves together and gave them psychological liberation which allowed them to express themselves fully. It granted them a feeling of human dignity required to survive. Hollywood movies have portrayed religion as something savage or primitive and have completely ignored its rich history.

Voodoo in Haiti Post Revolution

It is after the independence of Haiti that Voodooists were able to fully express themselves and follow their religion without any censorship or control. Haiti was one of the wealthiest colonies for France, and it was a blow for the powerful European country.

For the first time Slaves in Haiti were free to practice their religion which is why if one visits Haiti today, they can find an active community of Voodooists living unlike other parts of the Americas like New Orleans, known as the hub for Voodooists in America.

There are many monuments for the freedom of Voodoo in Haiti. Even though the country identifies as being Roman

Catholic, Voodoo is still the main religion of the country. Haiti is the motherland for all Voodooist, and if anyone wants to know more about the faith, then they should visit the tiny country.

FOUR

Voodoo and Racism

It seems like Voodoo and racism go hand in hand. Voodoo is one of the world's oldest religions dating all the way back to the time of Moses and the great Magi. It is more than just a religion and is more of a way of life. Voodoo is a religion followed by many in the Americas, the Caribbean and throughout the world.

The religion has an exciting history and is said to have entered the Americas on the arrival of Western African slaves who had been transported from Africa by European Colonial masters as a source of cheap labor. These slaves had been tortured and treated even worse than animals. The European Colonial masters were cruel with their treatment of slaves and didn't also allow them to live in their homes but to sleep in a sort of a barn outside the house with animals.

European hypocrisy is not something one must forget as Voodoo is a religion which has faced severe persecution. The new slaves who were brought in from Western Africa were forcefully converted by the Europeans and forced to accept Christianity even though they followed a Voodoo religion in countries like Nigeria and the Congo.

Inhumane Racism

These Western African slaves went through inhumane racism for their religion and practically had no rights they could not get out of slavery and were abused as well as raped by their European masters who were never held accountable for their crimes.

To understand Voodoo better, one needs first to gain an understanding of its history. It was Voodoo which brought the slaves together and gave them psychological solace which was even denied to them.

Abused throughout History

The followers of Voodoo or rather Voodooists have been abused throughout history for their beliefs. Many people of the Christian faith had a misconception that Voodooists worshipped Satan and offered animal sacrifices in his name even though it is the Abrahamic religions which practice something much similar as observed in Islam, Christianity, and Judaism. There is some form of animal sacrifice which is also required from them.

Europeans often mythologized and thought of the Voodooists as occultists or cannibals even though there have never been any signs of such. Voodooists were abused severely and made to do things which one can't also expect from animals.

More than You Think

Voodoo isn't what one might think it to be. It has been falsely portrayed in movies, television shows, and even books. Documentaries claiming to offer the truth about Voodoo are usually misleading as they only want to cash in on the views which have been set by Hollywood. Voodoo isn't a religion of devil worship or black magic.

Don't confuse Voodooists with sorcerers, witchdoctors or occultists. The religion isn't about hurting or controlling anyone, and it is rare for a Voodooist to have even seen a Voodoo doll.

The Role of the Media

The media is to blame for the existing views people have of Voodoo. The religion is never taken seriously and is only used by the media to make a quick buck. These same platforms should be held accountable for the role they play in increasing the racism which Voodooists go through.

Despite, the hundreds of years of abuse which Voodooists have gone through, even today they go through similar abuse.

Understand Voodoo

Voodoo originates from Africa but has since mixed with Catholicism and Native American traditions. It is difficult to estimate the number of followers the religion has today due to it not being recognized as a dominant religion by many countries even though the Catholic Church has identified the religion after persecuting it for many years.

The religion does not have a world authority and nor does it have any scripture. It is more focused on individual experience and is based around an individual's community. It is practiced differently throughout the world as in places like Haiti or New Orleans. In Haiti, Voodoo is the dominant religion practiced by the majority of the population. The religion embraces everyone and focuses on the entirety of human experience. People who want to follow their own religion or believe that they are imperfect find solace in the faith.

End Racism by Knowing What Voodooists Believe In

The Voodooists believe in two different worlds that is to say the visible and invisible world which is thought to be connected to one another and death is how one transition from one to the next. The ancestors who have passed away are believed to be with us while we are alive through their spirit.

Just like any other Monotheistic religion, Voodooists also believe in one God and have a belief in different Saints and Spirits known as Loa who provide guidance and safety to individuals.

Religion is more focused on individual human experience.

Possession is through as something right because it means that you have been connected to the invisible world and will better able to find guidance and enlightenment.

Freedom

Voodooists fought for their lives as was observed in the 18th century when the slaves in Haiti came together under a Voodoo Priestess to stand up against European Colonial masters and after a few years of fighting found freedom from France. It was the first country in Latin America to be free from European colonizers. It is after their independence that the African slaves in Haiti were free from racism.

Rest of the Americas

In countries like the United States, Voodooists still go through racism due to the presence of Fundamental Christians who have made the lives of Voodooists hard but denying them their rights and treating them as third class citizens.

Put an End to Voodoo Racism

It is through the understanding of the religion and its history can we put an end to Voodoo racism. One needs to show their support for the oppressed community to empower them and give them the freedom they deserve and have been fighting for years. Voodoo racism needs to be addressed accordingly.

FIVE

How Voodoo Influenced Hoodoo

Voodoo is a religion which has incorporated many aspects of Catholicism due to the famous practitioner Marie Laveau. It includes various prayers to its Angels, Saints and even combines the use of candles, holy water, and incense. The practices can be traced all the way back to the time of Moses and even the great Magi.

A Voodoo altar wouldn't be complete without a Bible. Much like Hoodoo practices. Psalms are regularly used in rituals. Religion is practical and not philosophical. Voodoo is similar to Hoodoo and is even called Hoodoo due to the use of magical traditions and its concern with daily life.

Belief in One God

Just like other major monotheistic religions like Christianity, Islam, and Judaism, Voodoo is only focused on one God and in man spirits referred to as Loa who act as spiritual helpers. These intercessors are said to carry messages to God. There is also a massive belief in ancestral spirits who are supposed to be with the family members even after their death.

Voodoo Influenced Hoodoo

Voodoo and Hoodoo are similar and can even be termed as one single religion, but the ideas surrounding the beliefs vary from place to place. Healing, protection, success, love, and money are at the core of both Voodoo and Hoodoo.

Magical Tradition

Voodoo and Hoodoo bear little resemblance to the African spirituality since Creoles and Europeans have contributed a lot to the religion, especially magical traditions. The beliefs have been influenced by a diverse mixture of Anglo, French, Spanish, African and American Indian religions and ideology. Hoodoo is the low magic cousin of Voodoo and is more focused in the New Orleans culture.

People of all ethnicities have been drawn to religion due to their practices. Voodooists and Hoodooists mostly seek spiritual guidance and healing. The doctrine focuses on a life of live and let live philosophy.

One of the Oldest Religions

Voodoo is considered to be one of the world's oldest religions and is of thought of the most potent religion with regards to the use of magic. It is practiced throughout the world and not just in New Orleans or the Americas.

Voodoo and Hoodoo quickly became popular in the Old West with many Voodoo societies still being in place today. There are some societies which allow outsiders to join the religion and learn about its magical powers.

Influence from African Americans

Hoodoo has strong ties with the African American community and their struggle for freedom. Western Africans have significantly influenced the religion with their native customs. Slaves that were brought in from Western Africa influenced the religion greatly. Voodoo and Hoodoo are both derived from African Voodoo. Even though New Orleans loves to claim that it is the center of Voodoo and Hoodoo, but it is African culture which has influenced both significantly.

There are some Asian influences as well on religion but not as strong as those of African culture. Voodoo paved the way for Hoodoo to become more popular.

SIX

Myths and Facts of Voodoo

Voodoo is a religion which has been around for a long time but has been a fetish for many. Voodooists have lived in fear throughout history due to the existence of Fundamental Christians who have wrongly associated the religion with black magic or Satanism.

Voodoo came into being in the Americas in the 18th century due to the arrival of West African refugees who brought with them their religion, but once these slaves arrived, they were forcefully converted by Christians. The evil image which has been promoted by the media about the ideology is untrue. The religion consists of several gods who are worshiped. Hollywood has shown a wrong depiction of the religion making it one of the most misunderstood religions. Here are a few of the myths and facts surrounding Voodoo.

Myth 1: Use Voodoo Dolls

One of the most popular myths which people like to believe about Voodoo is that Voodooists use Voodoo dolls which is only far from the truth. Voodoo dolls are much more complicated than portrayed in movies as it doesn't necessarily symbolize a person.

Myth 2: Satanic Religion

Another common myth among people is that Voodoo is an evil religion, whereas, different gods are believed in the spirituality, none of which is Behemoth himself.

Myth 3: Zombies

Thanks to Hollywood, everyone believes that Voodoo is all about zombies and that Voodooists control zombies which are profoundly untrue.

Myth 4: Few Adherents

A myth which people like to think is true is that there are few adherents of the religion, whereas, it is a significant religion in Haiti and it has followers throughout the world, even in the United States.

Myth 5: Evil

People think that Voodoo is an evil religion, even though the religion focuses on community and family.

Fact 1: Mix of Three Religions

Voodoo of today is a mix of three religions namely West African religion, Catholicism and Native American religion. These three religions gave birth to Voodoo.

Fact 2: Different Types of Voodoo

There isn't a single type of Voodoo, but there are three main types of Voodoo such as West African Voodoo which is practiced by over 30 million people, Louisiana Voodoo which is mostly practiced in New Orleans and Haitian Voodoo practiced as a dominant religion of the country.

Fact 3: Voodoo Followers are Servants to Spirits

The Voodoo religion believes in the existence of spirits, and the followers of the teachings are considered as servants to these spirits.

Fact 4: Accepted by the Catholic Church

Early in the 18th century, the Catholic Church came into contact with the Voodoo religion when European Colonial masters brought Western African slaves to the Americans for slave labor, and due to this, the Catholic Church accepts the belief.

Fact 5: Healing

Even though many people believe that Voodoo is evil, the religion in actuality focuses on the healing of individuals with the help of herbal medicines and spirits. The religion is centered on healing due to its dark history.

SEVEN

Voodoo Temples

Rituals usually take place in Voodoo temples, recognized as houmfor or hounfort. It is a considerably large half open space. At its center is a beam or pole where the God and spirits interact with the communities. Typically, the hounfort is decorated with esoteric paintings on the walls and highly decorated ceilings. It's highly decorated altar displays candles, pictures of Christian saints, symbolic items linked to the Loa. There is a feast before the service, and they create a specific Veve from flour or cornmeal relating to the Loa being worshiped is outlined on the temple's floor.

Dancing and chanting are begun by either or both the Houngan or Mambo and the students studying Vodoun known as hounsis. Accompanied by beats from rattles and religious drums called Tamboulas begins. The Loa possess one of the dancers. His or her ti bon ange, or soul, has left their body and the spirit has seized control. The dancer begins a trance and performs just as the Loa would.

An animal, this may be a goat, pig, sheep, or chicken, is sacrificed. The sacrificed animal's blood is collected in a vessel. Followers need this to gratify the hunger of the Loa. The possessed dancer may consume some of the animal's blood.

The appetite of the Loa need to be satisfied, which is understood. The animal is cooked and eaten by the followers. Animal sacrifice is blessing food for consumption by members of Voodoo, their gods and ancestors.

Besides being a place where sacred ceremonies are carried out, hounforts also function as communes. Attached to the Houngan or Mambo, the hounsis usually put in a significant amount of time at the hounfort.

The Houngan

The Houngan is the priest of voodoo, its spiritual leader. The Houngan acts as a community leader as well as a religious leader, and he serves many functions within the society. His maintains ultimate authority over the community because he is the only man who is thoroughly educated to connect with the gods and to translate the complex body of knowledge that makes up voodoo.

Houngans are deeply honored members of the community, someone who can be relied upon to provide sensible advice, with all the force of the spirit world behind it. Virtually nothing is done in the community without first turning to the Houngan. The Houngan has many steps by which to connect to the Loas, including dreams, ritual invocation, and fortune-telling using cards, palm-reading, or figure sketches.

Each society's spiritual leader also possesses the authority to modify the voodoo ceremonies of his community, adapting them to the specific gods that are revered by that community, which reveals why voodoo practices can differ so considerably even in centers that are right next door to each other. The same as a priest, the Houngan serves as confessor, confidential counselor, economic consultant, and prophet for the individuals in his neighborhood.

Commonly, the Houngan obtains his position from his father or other male relative. The present Houngan prepares future priests from a young age, and the new Houngan is not fully initiated until he enters his early thirties, often at the age of thirty-one.

The Mambo

A fully initiated female priestess in the Voodoo religion is recognized as a Mambo. A Mambo is equal in every relation to her male counterpart, a Houngan. She summons Voodoo Loas to foresee the future or to heal.

These priestesses are the heads of independent church groups, rather than clerical hierarchies. Mambos exercise their authority over the followers or spiritual assistants in their temples.

Although Voodoo spirits can incarnate themselves in whomever they prefer, the intimacy offered to the followers does not include direct links with the spirits or gods.

Mambos, on the other hand, have the proficiencies needed to communicate to and hear from the Voodoo spirits. The powers contained in mambos reside in their knowledge or konesans. Frequently referred to as intuition, psychic energy, or the gift of sight, Voodoo priestesses can read people and heal them. This, in turn, allows them to diagnose and treat human sufferings, which they believe can stem from the living, the dead, or the spirit world.

Mambos receive a vocational education where they learn about the various Voodoo spirits and ritualistic practices. They also have inherent talent or knowledge which can differ from one another. Because the scope of their konesans ultimately stems from supernatural abilities, the Voodoo Loas choose the mambos either through the revelations of a dream or the utterances of a possessed person.

EIGHT

The Loas

In the New World Voodoo, the spirits or Loas are forces of nature. Divided into three major groups, Rada, Petro, and Ghede, they are extensions of the power of Bondye, the Supreme Cosmic God, and the whole doctrine of the universe. We do not revere the Loa as Gods. We serve them so that in turn they help us. They serve as mediators between individuals and Bondye. It is realistic to state that the Loa are ancestors.

The belief of Voodoo, as practiced in New Orleans, is continuously growing, shifting, continually adding new Loas to the shrine or pantheon. As such, American spirits and ancestors have come to be accepted as influential Loas in their own right, specifically such warriors or heroes as the Native Americans Black Hawk and White Hawk, and other Loas who resided and passed in New Orleans, like Marie Laveau and Doctor John.

Because there are literally thousands of Loas, only the most prominent and best-known are described below. Worship of these Loas can be discovered elsewhere throughout the United States, but for the most part, these personalities are recognized notably in New Orleans, Louisiana.

Rada Loa Spirits

The Rada Loa are typically older, more beneficent as many of these spirits come from Africa. The Rada Loas are mainly water spirits, so many of the Rada Loas generally are served with water. In addition to their colors, these were spirits were honored by slaves who were captured and transported to the New World. The Rada became the main spirits within the later religion synthesized. Rada Loas features identify with the color white. Their holy day is Thursday.

Rada Loas are regularly believed also to have Petro aspects. Sources describe these distinct identities as aspects, while others interpret them as separate beings.

Agwe

Agwe is the Loa who symbolizes the sea. He is the protector of fishermen and sailors.

Offerings to Agwe consists of champagne, liqueurs, coffee with sugar and cream, cakes, white wine, white sheep, white ram goats, white roosters, model ships, cane syrup, rice cooked in coconut milk, melons, boiled cornmeal, fried ripe bananas, and ducks.

Rituals for Agwe are held near the sea, loaded on small, specially constructed small boats or rafts and set adrift at sea. If the vessel sinks, you know your sacrifice has been accepted.

His colors are white, sea green and blue. With Thursdays, August 30 and 31st being Agwe's sacred days.

Boats, small metal fishes, paddles are his symbols, while he is associated with Lake Ponchartrain, Bayou St. John, and the Mississippi River.

Agwe's Catholic counterpart is Saint Ulrich or Saint Expedite.

Ayida Wedo

Wife of Damballa, Ayida Wedo is the Loa of fertility and new life. Being known as the Rainbow Snake, she takes a snake form.

Ayida Wedo shares her husband with his mistress, Erzulie Freda, the Loa of romantic love.

Offerings to Ayida-Wedo consist of rice pudding whipped cream rice, eggs, and milk. Basically, she craves white foods even sweetened café au lait with lots of milk. Offerings in the form of snakes, rainbows, or adorned with a rainbow motif are much appreciated.

Ayida-Wedo's colors are deep blue and white, with her sacred days being

The Rainbow is Ayida-Wedo symbol; so naturally, she's associated with water and the cotton tree (Ceiba pentandra).

Ayida-Wedo's Catholic counterpart is Our Lady of Immaculate Conception.

Ayizan

Being the root Loa of business and economics, Ayizan is also the protector of the Houngan as well as religious ceremonies. During these rituals, Ayizan is a Loa who never possesses anyone.

As the wife of Loko, she is seen as the first priestess and is associated with that priestly knowledge and mysteries. Especially the understanding of initiation and the natural world itself. Ayizan is the moral governess of humankind, helping us to balance our desire for pleasure with guilt.

Combine Ayizan's mental side with fortune-telling a traditional Mardi Gras activity. Use your own palm for divination if you don't have a palm leaf available.

Even with Mardi Gras, Ayizan drinks no alcohol. Offerings to Ayizan consists of palm hearts, white yams (basically white foods), and bananas

Her colors are White, silver, gold, and yellow.

Palm fronds are her symbols, while she is associated with ancestors, commerce, Mambos, priestesses healing, initiation, and palm trees.

Ayizan's Catholic counterpart is Saint Claire.

Damballa

Damballa is one of the most prominent of all the Loas. Damballa is the Sky Father and the inherent designer of all living things. Similar to his wife Ayida-Weddo, Damballa is represented as a snake, and both Loas are regarded to be some of the wisest. In command of the equilibrium inside the cosmos, Damballa rules over the soul and intelligence. He inspires peace and unity throughout the universe.

He is a protector to the hurt, lame, wounded and his appearance in the world is a giant snake using his 7,000 spirals to produce the stars and the planets in the skies and to form the mountains and valleys on earth while his shed skin produced the oceans, rivers, and lakes.

Although Damballa is married to Ayida-Weddo, his mistress is no other than Erzulie Freda.

Offerings to Damballa consists of coconut, coconut milk, honey, syrup, rice, mild cigars, white cakes, salt, cold water, milk, white egg on a rounded pile of white flour, Shea butter, bread, and cookies.

His color is white, with April 27th, July 16th, August 25th and Thursdays as his sacred days.

Naturally, snakes are his symbol as well as white cloths, owls and chameleons. Damballa is associated with the cotton tree, Ceiba pentandra.

Damballa's Catholic counterparts are Moses and St. Patrick.

Erzulie Freda

Erzulie Freda is the most beloved of the Loas. The Loa of love, beauty, purity, Erzulie Freda is the representation of the ideal female. In honor of her three husbands, Erzulie Freda wears three wedding rings.

Always made up, perfumed and adorns with all manner of jewelry, Erzulie Freda can influence romance, marriage, good fortune, and artistic endeavors.

Even with Erzulie Freda being femininity and compassion

embodied, she also has a darker side. She is sometimes seen as spoiled, jealous and is considered to be lazy.

Offerings to Erzulie Freda consists of perfume, make-up, pink champagne, rich and luxurious foods, gold jewelry, soap, white towels, cakes, puddings, rice cooked in milk and cinnamon, pink and white cakes, basil, Florida water, and pink flowers.

Her colors are white, pink, and pale blue with Thursdays and July 16th as her sacred days.

Hearts and a white lantern or lamps with a white bulb are Erzulie Freda's symbols, while she is associated with white doves and laurel trees.

The Catholic counterparts to Erzulie Freda are Our Lady of Lourdes, Mater Dolorosa de Monte Calvario and Our Lady of Sorrows.

La Sirene

Seen as a mermaid, La Sirene is a facet of Erzulie who represents the sea.

Offerings to La Sirene consists of sweet white wine white rum, white cakes decorated in blue, white doves, champagnes, gin, melon liqueur, melons, molasses, desserts, and perfume.

La Sirene colors are pale blue, aquamarine and white with February 2, December 8 and Thursdays being her sacred days.

For this Loa, seashells, mirrors, combs, and trumpets are her symbols. La Sirene is associated with the Moon, the number seven and the seven seas.

The Catholic counterparts to La Sirene are La Diosa Del Mar, St. Martha, Nuestra Senora de la Caridad, and Our Lady of the Seafaring.

Papa Legba

Papa Legba is one of the most well-known Loa. He is considered the gate-keeper to the Loa world. He stands at a spiritual junction or crossroad and grants or denies permission to converse with the spirits of the spirit world known as Guinee. He's customarily one of the first last Loa requested during a Voodoo ritual. Despite his power and influence, Legba is commonly perceived as an old man, usually with scars or disfigurements.

Donning a straw hat and smoking a pipe, Papa Legba utilizes a crutch or cane to walk, with his straw sack with him to carry his contributions. He's a moderately amicable person but can additionally be a bit of a joker or trickster.

Voodoo practitioners set representations of Papa Legba behind the front door of their home to unblock the path, achieve goals, and to bring his protection.

Offerings to Papa Legba consists of sweet potatoes, grilled chicken, plantains, a small bag with a bottle of Kleren inside, bones, tobacco and a pipe hanging from a tree or doorway.

Papa Legba's sacred days are June 13th and Thursdays with red and white being his colors.

Associated with Calabash trees; walking stick, crutches, dogs, roosters, keys, and crosses are Papa Legba's symbols.

St. Lazarus, St. Peter and St. Anthony of Padua are his Catholic counterparts.

Petro Loa Spirits

The Petro Loas are mostly the more intense, sometimes aggressive and warlike Loas and are linked frequently with darker subjects and practices. Having originated in the New World, they do not occur in African Vodou practices.

Petro Loas will only work for someone if the devotee makes a promise of service to them, which often requires an expensive sacrifice, and the god will take revenge if that promise isn't kept. Petro rituals are characterized by red formal clothing; off-beat syncopated drumming, and frenzied dancing.

Invocation of any Petro Loas always means risking damage of body and spirit. They work quickly, and they don't play around. Therefore, those not adequately prepared for such actions should avoid it altogether.

Their Holy day is Tuesday, and their colors tend to be fiery red.

Erzulie Dantor

The darker aspect of Erzulie. Erzulie Dantor is the Loa of jealousy and vengeance and is often cruel. Her veve is the heart pierced by a dagger which perfectly depicts her nature.

Offerings to Erzulie Dantor consists of roasted and seasoned griyot (fried pork), black female Creole pigs, black hens, rice with pigeon peas, sweet potatoes, yams, red wine steeped with herbs, Kleren, beer, Barbancourt rum, dark and robust filter less cigarettes, cigars, daggers, dolls, silver jewelry, Florida water, and musky perfume.

Her colors are red, navy blue and gold, with July 16, August 15 and Tuesdays being Erzulie Dantor's sacred days.

A blue paket Kongo, black dolls, and a bowl of blood with knives, are her symbols while being associated with New Orleans.

Erzulie Dantor Catholic counterparts are St. Barbara Africana, Mater Salvatoris, Our Lady of Mount Carmel, Black Madonna of Czestochowa, St. Joan of Arc and Our Lady of Perpetual Help.

Grand Bois

A Loa of the wilderness, Grand Bois, is the master of nature. An elemental, Grand Bois is attuned to the earth and the forest, closely linked with herbs, plants, trees, and trees. Half-man and half-tree with a stout, Grand Bois has a trunk-like body, branches for fingers plus roots for feet.

Grand Bois is a powerful magician since he is part of the Triad of Magicians. He stands alongside stands Baron Cimetiere and Mait' Carrefour.

Offerings to Grand Bois are sweet potatoes, yams, green bananas, cornmeal, peanut cakes, cassava bread black pigs, goats, Kleren, cornmeal, distilled rum, as well as any type of food from the forests, such as leaves, flowers, wild berries, and acorns.

Grand Bois' colors are red, green, and brown. Strangely formed pieces of wood or roots are his symbols.

Associated with Mapou trees, the Catholic counterparts to Grand Bois are St. Christopher and St. Sebastian.

Mait' Carrefour

Mait' Carrefour is Papa Legba's dark twin some Voodoo practitioners see them as the same deity, the Loa themselves know the truth. Just as Papa Legba rules the benevolent spirits of the day Mait' Carrefour is the master of the evil spirits of the night.

Standing on opposite sides of all doorways and on opposite corners of all crossroads, wherever you find one, the other is at no time far away. Also, their outfits are similar. The only way to tell the difference between them is to view them carefully. Mait' Carrefour's attire is more tone down in color than Papa Legba's.

People do not talk in Mait' Carrefour's company. When he arrives at a ceremony, everyone in attendance will stop talking because he permits evil Loas to come to the service.

Mait' Carrefour is the grand master of charms and sorceries and is closely associated with black magic. Ceremonies for him are frequently held at the crossroads.

Mait' Carrefour's offerings is a drink of rum infused with gunpowder. Associated with the night, crossroads, and the Moon, you'll find the Moon is also his symbol.

With his sacred day Tuesday, Mait' Carrefour's color is red with Satan being his Catholic counterpart.

Marinette

A demigoddess who in her mortal life was a Mambo. Marinette sacrificed a black pig at the start of the First Haitian Revolution. After dying as a martyr, Marinette was raised to the station of a Loa. While she is extremely violent and vicious, Marinette cannot indeed be called an evil Loa, as she is one who releases her people from slavery or pulls them back into it.

Her followers do not have altars to her but go to such places to bury her offerings. She, in turn, will appear and dig them up, consuming them under a mask of darkness so that she is not required to split her prize with any other Loa. Mambo Marinette is revered in these wild places where salt, dust, and gasoline are flung onto a bonfire in exchange for the bony lady's aid with malicious magic.

Mambo Marinette is not cruel. She only gets brutal in possession and if somebody burns animals or humans.

Like most Loas, Marinette is partnered with one who is thought to be similar to her, if a bit less cruel, Ti-Jean Petro.

An offering to Marinette consists of sweets, lavender, black pigs or black roosters who are plucked alive.

Marinette's sacred day is Tuesdays with her colors being blood red and black.

Screech owls are Marinette's symbols, and she is associated with Werewolves. The Anima Sola is Marinette's Catholic counterpart.

Ti-Jean Petro

Described as a dwarf with one foot, Ti-Jean Petro Is a New Orleans serpent spirit who dances in flames and consumes hot things when in possession of a human body. This Loa often protects and assists the sorcerers of black magic.

Ti-Jean Petro has a violent and dramatic nature that manifests when he has servants. He's perceived to inhale two Cigs at once, and similar to Baron Samedi, he enjoys wearing hats. He has healing and predictive capabilities. Ti-Jean Petro is wedded to Erzulie Dantor and Mambo Marinette.

Known as Petro-e-rouge, Ti-Jean-pied-fin, Prince Zandor, and Ti-Jean-Zandor, the traditional picture used for invocation is his Catholic counterpart, St. John the Baptist.

An offering to Ti-Jean Petro consists of grenadine syrup, a plate of sweets, fruit tartar, pastry, red cola, and cake.

Pale yellow is his colors while June 24, Tuesdays and

Saturdays are his sacred days. Ti-Jean Petro is also associated with the metal Silver.

Ghede Loa Spirits

Ghede Loas are identified with the dead and also with sensuality. They transport dead souls, act irreverently; perform dances that imitate sexual association. They celebrate life during death. They are intense defenders of children and can eliminate evil spirits and clear away evil work. Ghede Loas are also exceptionally valuable in healing work, and some situations can stop death. Their sacred day is typically Friday, and their traditional color is purple, black and white.

Baron Samedi

Being the Loa of the dead, Baron Samedi is the ultimate suave and sophisticated spirit of Death. Frequently represented with a black tuxedo, white top hat, set of dark glasses, and cotton plugs in the nostrils, Baron Samedi resembles a corpse dressed and prepared for burial. Talking through his nose, He has a white, skull-like face, and tells crude but funny jokes.

As the souls of humans pass on their way to Guinee, Baron Samedi stands at the crossroads. He is a protector of children and is often petitioned for sick children. He has control over zombies and determines whether or not people can be transformed into animals. Since Baron Samedi is the lord of death, he is the last resort for healing since he must decide whether to allow them to cross over or to enable them to recover.

Baron Samedi is also the Loa of resurrection and is called upon for healing by that near or approaching death. It is only Baron Samedi who can accept an individual into the realm of the dead and regulates the gate between the world of the living and the realm of the dead. He is thought to be a wise judge and a great magician.

As well as being the all-knowing Loa of death, he is a sexual Loa, frequently represented by phallic representations.

He is the head of the Guede family of Loa and married to the Loa Manman Brigit.

Baron Samedi is said to be most regularly summoned and found in St. Louis cemetery number one. His offerings are Kleren infused with hot peppers, black coffee, bread, rice and black beans, coconut meat, grilled corn, peanuts, everything heavily-seasoned with hot peppers black roosters, black goats, cigars, and cigarettes.

His colors are black, white, and purple, with November 1st, November 2nd, Mondays, and Saturdays as his sacred days.

Skulls, black crosses, coffins, a deck of cards, top hat, sunglasses missing one lens, shovels, cane or baton are his symbols, while he is associated with crossroads, magic, and Death.

Baron Samedi's Catholic counterpart is St. Martin de Porres.

Maman Brigitte

Maman Brigitte is a death Loa as well as the wife of Baron Samedi. Recognized as Lover of Bones, Lady of the Cemetery, Maman Brigitte is a protector, spiritual matron, and one of the Guede. Maman Brigitte is one of the most potent Loas, offering protection to cemeteries and the deceased. Frequently viewed as a Corpse Bride, Maman Brigitte calls upon us to deal with both our mortality and our ancestral descents.

She inspires us to reach out, and take ownership of our destinies, rather than "going with the flow," and thus living and loving life while we can. An aspect of the Divine Feminine who is not to be feared, Maman Brigitte offers to us the chance to deal with our mortality head-on, as well as to genuinely embrace and cherish our bones.

As the Loa of wealth, appeal to Maman Brigitte for support in financial matters, especially those of probates and wills. She commands that we thoroughly know and respect the sacredness of these transactions.

Maman Brigitte is recognized as corresponding to other women of the Dead or Underworld, such as Persephone, Hel or Hecate. Her aspect is that of changes, and of guarding the graveyards and the interred remains, rather than overseeing the land of the dead itself. Maman Brigitte protects properly marked gravestones in cemeteries. These markers would bear a cross on them. She will punish those who fail to respect or care for the deceased, and can be threatening in correcting such sins.

Offerings to Maman Brigitte consists of roasted peanuts, roasted corn, spicy food, rice with black beans, Kleren infused with 21 hot peppers, rum, black coffee, black chickens, bread, coconut meat, sweet potatoes, smoked mackerel, and filter less cigarettes.

Maman Brigitte's colors are purple, black and white. November 1st, November 2nd, Mondays, and Saturdays are her sacred days.

The Scales of Justice and crosses are her symbols while she is associated with the number nine.

The Catholic counterpart to Maman Brigitte is St. Brigid.

Various New Orleans Loa and Spirits
Black Hawk

Black Hawk is an Indian Spirit Guide who has a significant influence on Hoodoo and Voodoo today. His likeness can be seen on many hoodoo products such as Indian Spirit Incense and room spray.

A renowned chief and warrior of the Native American Sauk tribe, Black Hawk lived from 1767 to 1838. Born "Ma-ka-tai-me-she-kia-kiak," He was not a hereditary chief; instead, he had been appointed a war chief for his cunning leadership and ferocity in battle.

Wanting to force white American colonists away from the Sauk nation, Black Hawk had fought on the side of the British during the War of 1812, against the U.S. Afterward, he led a party of Sauk and Fox warriors, identified as the British Band, against European-American immigrants in Illinois and what is known today as Wisconsin in the 1832 Black Hawk War. After the war, he was taken by U.S. forces and brought to the eastern U.S.

At the end of his life, he attempted conciliation with both the whites and rival Sauk warriors. In the Native American tradition, Black Hawk is an elder. Elders are revered and given the utmost respect.

The 1920s, Black Hawk, was introduced into Spiritualist and hoodoo practices in New Orleans by Mother Leafy Anderson, a leader in the Spiritual Church Movement. It is likely that during her childhood in Wisconsin, she first became acquainted with the history of Black Hawk, later coming to accept him as a spirit guide.

Black Hawk is often called upon for spells of protection and warding off enemies, and he is described as a watcher on the wall considering he would send signs of any breaking through in spiritual welfare. He can also be called upon for money, to assure justice in private matters and court cases, and many people of Native American descent pay homage to him as a way to connect with and honor their lost tribal ancestors.

Black Hawk is petitioned by the individual in their homes. He is typically evoked for help with money and protection, justice, release from prison, to win court cases and overcome tragedy, as well as any problem you may be facing. He is the consummate warrior and wants to fight your battles for you. They say he will come to those who have enough patience to sit still and listen.

Offering to Black Hawk consists of tobacco, fruit, bread spaghetti and meatballs, red beans and rice.

A bucket filled with dirt or sand within which stands a statuette of a Native American is Black Hawk's symbol with Wednesdays and Sundays being his sacred days.

Having no specific color or Catholic counterparts, Black Hawk is associated with protection, justice, and war.

Simbi

As a Loa of rainfall and fresh water, Simbi oversees the making of charms using white magic. One of the three universal serpents of New Orleans voodoo religion, Simbi is the water snake Loa and can do nothing without water.

He is a well-informed Loa because he spends a lot of time learning about the nature of supernatural diseases and how to treat them. He protects those who have good relations with him and denies those who do not. Simbi also provides a specific connection between people and ghosts, because among voodoo people the mythical other side is buried in the sea.

Decorate his altar with pictures of snakes, divination tools and magical devices.

Being a water snake, Simbi needs to stay wet. He accepts water, particularly spring water, rainwater, or pond water, or milk. Mangos, yams, ribbons, and shed snakeskins. He drinks alcoholic beverages like whiskey or rum. Snakes don't like the cold so Simbi may prefer refreshments served at room temperature. He may wish to have access to various beverages simultaneously.

Green, white, gray are Simbi's colors as well as Mondays, Tuesdays, Thursdays, Fridays, or Saturdays being his sacred days.

Simbi is associated with the crystal Quartz, river rocks, the metal Mercury, elm, Calabash as well as turtles, and other snakes.

Sousson Pannan

In Voodoo of New Orleans Sousson-Pannan is an ugly and evil Loa whose body is covered with sores. Sousson-Pannan is known to drink copious amounts of blood and liquor.

St. Expedite

Saint Expedite is a mighty and fast acting folk saint famous in New Orleans among Voodooists and mainstream

Catholics alike. His help is likewise petitioned by those that want to conquer procrastination as a particular harmful habit, as well as by sailors, retailers, and businesspersons.

Very little is specific as to the history of this saint, but he has been revered for many years, since the Middle Ages. One of the more well-known stories tells that Expeditus was a Roman centurion who lived in Armenia and became a Christian. On the day of his conversion, Satan supposedly took the form of a crow and tried to tempt him from his path by telling him to delay his baptism for another day. Expeditus stamped upon the crow and killed it, stating that he would be a Christian today. During the Diocletian Persecution in 303 A.D., he was beheaded and declared a martyr.

Expedite is generally depicted as a youthful Roman centurion holding up a cross marked HODIE, Latin for "today," as he's stepping on a crow beneath his right foot. From the crow's mouth appears a ribbon with the word CRAS, Latin for "tomorrow." Consequently Expedite ends a questionable tomorrow in support of a promised today.

Another tale of the Saint's story begins in New Orleans. The Chapel of Our Lady of Guadalupe once received a box of unlabeled saint statuettes. Without a name or description to identify the saint figurines, no one knew which saint they were for. But, on the front, there was a label that said: "Expedite." The citizens then concluded that Expedite was the saint's name, and to this day, he continues to be included predominantly in local Creole folklore and is revered through prayers and offerings.

Whatever the roots of this saint, there is no doubt that Saint Expedite is powerful and answers requests promptly. If there is a service of which you are in urgent need, offering assistance to Saint Expedite may help to manifest it quickly. Saint Expedite is not a standard Voodoo spirit, and he is not of African origin, so his service is a bit varied and less complicated.

St. Expedite's offerings are pound cakes, flowers, and water, with his color being red.

Naturally, the cross and palm leaf are St. Expedite's symbols. He is associated with the metal mercury.

Celebrate his feast day April 19th and his sacred day is Wednesdays.

There are no Catholic counterparts to St. Expedite, but he has been often linked with Mercury/Hermes.

Li Grande Zombi

Li Grande Zombi is the all-powerful serpent spirit of reverence among New Orleans Voodooists. They are symbols of wisdom and holders of intuitive, mystical knowledge, things that cannot be spoken. When women dance with the serpent In New Orleans, it is a symbol of the balance between the two genders. The snake represents masculine energy, dancing in harmony with the feminine power of the priestess. Voodoo rituals in New Orleans almost always include a snake dance to celebrate the link to this sacred and ancient knowledge.

The name of this Loa is most commonly linked to the name of Marie Laveau's pet snake which was a large Ball Python. Some say she kept the snake in a box at the foot of her bed; other accounts say that she kept the snake in a box under the bed, and still another report claims she didn't have a snake at all

The most significant way to acknowledge Li Grand Zombi is with a live snake. This is not a responsibility to be embarked upon lightly. Taking accountability as well as responsibility for a pet is no small undertaking, mainly when that pet is also a spirit animal. While snakes are relatively low-maintenance companions, they have specific requirements which must be met. If not given suitable temperatures and moisture, they are apt to grow ill and die.

Reportedly, St John's Eve June 23 the day when the biggest Voodoo gathering Li Grande Zombi was worshipped at Marie Laveau's New Orleans Voodoo rituals on Bayou St. John every year. It is also the day that many followers insist the ghost of Marie Laveau arises from the dead. To this day, it is still the most critical Voodoo holiday in New Orleans. But, Li Grande Zombi did not begin or end with Marie Laveau.

A snake which is going to be manipulated in a public ritual also demands to have a well docile temperament. Remember, even the most docile snake may respond by biting when stressed or musking or defecating on the nearest convenient mark. That large python you are dancing with may be less exciting when you are nursing a bloody open wound or covered with runny snake dung. The responsibility of your own special Grand Zombi is past the range of this writing. I am an animal lover and as with any other pet, do your due diligence and research before making your investment. Be sure you are able to live up to your obligation. There is no shame in admitting if you are unable to do so at this time.

Shed snakeskin can additionally be utilized as offerings for Grand Zombi, in addition to snake figures or representation. Please do not use snakeskins considering they are collected by killing the snakes. What a way to anger him by offering him the corpse of a brother or sister. Show your commitment and establish a link with Li Grand Zombi by adding offerings of eggs, candles or if you are rhythmically talented, try drumming.

Azaca-Tonnerre

Loa of thunder agriculture and protector of the crops, Azaca-Tonnerre is pictured as a peasant carrying a straw bag called a macoute.

Offerings to Azaca-Tonnerre consists of sweet potatoes, salted cod, boiled corn, yams, rice and beans, cola, Kleren steeped in certain herbs, tequila, cane syrup, sugar cane, coffee with a lot of sugar, cassava bread, bananas, fruit, hard candy, popcorn mixed with coconut, toasted corn and peanuts, and a red rooster.

Always smoking tobacco in a pipe, his colors are denim, white, and green.

Azaca-Tonnerre's Catholic counterpart is St. Isidore.

Marassa

Marassa is the sacred twins who are saluted in every ritual. Thought to have stability and be two parts of the same whole, Marassa signifies aggressive male and passive female energy. The twins symbolize the sun and the moon. Together they create a hermaphrodite deity that symbolizes inseparable divine unity. Twins, mainly if it is a girl and a boy are thought as their mortal representatives.

They are thought to be orphans without good food discipline. They eat everything offered to them from twin dishes, always coming very hungry for the ceremonies. The twins must be fed until they are filled, so they will be content and will want to listen to people.

They are foreseen as difficult, impulsive, sensitive and malicious (mischievous, vicious) beings. They refuse to take responsibility for any harm or illness they cause.

In everyday life, it is recommended to deal with both children the same way, as they react in a compassionate approach to any differences made between them. Families with twins often suffer diseases or bad luck, which is explained among voodoo people that the family did not complete their duty to Marassa.

An offering to the Marassa consists of candy, cookies, honey, popcorn, toys, and fun, fizzy drinks. Be sure to wrap food up in banana leaves. Just remember, vegetables or leafy greens will insult them. They're children after all.

The Marassa's sacred days are December 28th, Mondays and Fridays, with their colors being black and white.

Associated with Palm leaves and branches, the Marassa's Catholic counterparts are St. Damian and St. Cosmas.

Loko

Loko is a facet of Legba that is master of the hounfort. In

the Voodoo religion, represents medicine, healers, and healing plants He is often invoked to help with healing and to protect against black magic.

As a Rada Loa, Loko is the husband of Loa Ayizan and is considered the first Houngan. As the spiritual parents of the priesthood, Loko and Ayizan are two of the Loa associated in the Kanzo initiation rites.

Offers for Loko are placed in straw bags which are then hung from its branches. Being the personification of plants, he is recognizable only by the pipe smoked by his servants and by the stick he holds in his hand.

Roosters are the main offerings for Loko. His colors are pale green, golden yellow, and white.

January 6th, May 1st, and Wednesdays are considered to be his sacred days, with his symbol being red roosters.

Loko is associated with the wind, butterflies, the number 41, and the Mapou tree (Cyphostemma mappia).

The Catholic counterparts to Loko are the Archangel Gabriel and St. Joseph.

Ogoun

Frequently called the Voodoo Hercules, Ogoun is the spirit of iron, war, fire, metalworking, and politics. Ogoun is believed to have come down to fight in every war in Haiti's history in various human guises. Ogoun is likewise thought to be the Father of technology.

He can be very argumentatively masculine but can control the head of the female, or emasculate male initiates to whom he takes affection.

Ogoun is also connected with blood and is for this purpose frequently requested to cure disorders of the blood. Those possessed by Ogoun smoke cigars, don red clothing and carry a sword or machete.

Offerings to Ogoun consists of a red rooster, smoked fish, yams, green plantains, sapodillas, rice with red beans, Barbancourt rum, cigars, young bulls, three railroad ties, black dogs, pigeons, toy cars, toy trains, toy planes, and toy weapons.

Depending on the facet, Ogoun's colors are green and black or Red and blue. June 29th, July 25th, Tuesdays and Wednesdays are his sacred days.

Ogoun's symbols are a sword driven into the earth, sabers, machetes, butterflies, red paket Kongo, red scarf and flags. He is associated with iron, blood, war, justice, locomotives, masculinity, number 7 and Calabash trees.

The Catholic counterparts to Ogoun are St. George and St. Jacques Majeur.

The Saints

The connections linking Voodoo and Catholicism are extraordinary. One of the trademarks of New Orleans Voodoo is the adding of components of Catholicism, particularly the saints. Each Loa is affiliated with a Catholic saint. Furthermore, the saints frequently present a more fundamental purpose than do the Loas in magic.

Using Damballa as an example, who is depicted as a serpent god and is closely associated with snakes. Damballa's Christian counterparts would be Moses, who changed a rod into a serpent in the Pharaoh's court and St. Patrick, who drove the snakes out of Ireland.

Once you understand and know the saints and their intention, you can design your own rituals to suit your need. Recognizing the saints, their associated meaning, and the corresponding Loa is vital to New Orleans Voodoo.

Remember, prayers to Saints aren't just for Catholics. Regardless of religion, prayers should motivate and influence you.

Guardian Angel - Protect yourself and children from danger and evil spirits by praying to the Guardian Angel.

Infant Jesus of Atocha - To be free from punishment, guilt, and sin, pray to the Infant Jesus of Atocha.

Miraculous Mother - To bring good things into your life, pray to the Miraculous Mother.

Our Lady of Charity - If you need protection for your home, bring in prosperity or find a lover, pray to Our Lady of Charity.

Our Lady of Guadalupe - Pray to Our Lady of Guadalupe when you need protection from curses or to overcome fear.

Our Lady of Mercy - For mental clarity, especially for during studies, pray to Our Lady of Mercy.

Our Lady of Perpetual Help - When you need help, pray to Our Lady of Perpetual Help.

Sacred Heart of Jesus - For a blessed, peaceful life, pray to Sacred Heart of Jesus.

Sacred Heart of Mary - For spiritual blessings and serenity, pray to Sacred Heart of Mary.

Seven African Powers or Saints - Pray to Seven African Powers or Saints to solve problems. This prayer is all-purpose.

St. Anthony of Padua - Pray to St. Anthony of Padua when something is lost.

St. Barbara - For love, friendship and to conquer enemies, pray to St. Barbara.

St. Bernadette - When healing is needed, pray to St. Bernadette.

St. Christopher - For protection during travel, pray to St. Christopher.

St. Dymphna - For demonic possession or mental disorders, pray to St. Dymphna.

St. Expedite - If you are in pressing need, pray to St. Expedite.

St. Joseph - Pray to St. Joseph to sell or rent a house or to find a job.

St. Jude - When you find yourself in impossible situations, pray to St. Jude.

St. Lazarus - For healing and sickness, pray to St. Lazarus.

St. Lucy - Suffering from writer's block? Pray to St. Lucy, the patron saint of writers.

St. Martin Caballero - If you're a business person wanting to draw in more customers, pray to St. Martin Caballero.

St. Martin De Porres - For comfort, health, friends, for a good life, pray to St. Martin De Porres.

St. Michael - To overcome obstacles, remove evil, and defeat your enemies, pray to St. Michael.

St. Peter - To open roads and bring you opportunities for success, pray to St. Peter.

St. Raphael - If you need healing from spiritual and physical ailments, pray to St. Raphael.

St. Rose - To open the doors to Paradise, pray to St. Rose. St. Rose will also grant women a more suitable boyfriend or husband.

St. Raymond - To silence your enemies and stop gossip and slander, pray to St. Raymond.

NINE

The Voodoo Queens

Sainte Dede

Before Voodoo Queen Marie Laveau, there was Sainte Dede. As a young woman from Santo Domingo (which is now Haiti), Sainte Dede, obtained her way to freedom in New Orleans, by buying her way out. Someone could find Dede, now a free woman of color, selling food near the Cabildo and in Place d'Armes.

There was no refuting that Sainte Dede had compiled a great deal of abundance for herself, being the ambitious spirit that she was. As she had gained enough in her Voodoo business as well as other sideline jobs, it was possible for her to have not merely got her freedom from slavery, but to have invested in a comfortable little home for herself there on the intersections of Rue Dumaine and Rue Chartres. It's said Sainte Dede lived better than some white families did.

Sainte Dede was one of the most revered names in New Orleans Voodoo cliques between 1803 and the 1820s. She would later be a teacher and mentor to the most famous voodoo queen, Marie Laveau. She would hold rituals in her yard just blocks away from the Cathedral. Parishioners could hear the rhythmic pulse of the drums during mass. For that reason in 1817, the church decided that they would not allow any religion was not Catholic to take place inside the limits of the city. Congo Square, presently Armstrong Park, was the area that the early Voodouns conducted their rituals. It describes her as running an integrated Voodoo religion as early as 1822. They published a detailed chronicle of one of her ceremonies in the publication Century. This account is unreliable, nevertheless, as the source was an adolescent boy who alleges to have been led to the service by one of his father's slaves. It recounts the usual Voodoo items being used (a black doll, a snake, a calabash), and a celebration of singing, dancing, drumming, and of course, possession.

The one thing the residents of New Orleans feared was a Voodoo curse! It is the gravest of all outcomes. Sinister magic in different segments of the country lessened in relation. Practitioners now will not do harmful magic, but back in 1944, it was a totally different vibe.

Madame Marie Laveau

Most people associate Voodoo with dolls and witchcraft. They visualize the images of needles being inserted into a doll when they first hear the word voodoo. Therefore, a negative image of voodoo is created and widespread. However, the reality, sometimes, may differ from the general perception; same is the case of Marie Laveau–the renowned voodoo queen of New Orleans.

Charles Laveau, A Creole man, and his mulatto lover Marguerite conceived a child with enormous supernatural gifts. She was destined to become a prominent seraphic in life and even a full-fledged goddess in passing, although no one truly grasped it.

Some people believe that Marie Laveau was born in 1801 while records that her birth year is 1794. Since she was from African, Native American and European ancestry, and existing at the period she did, they reared Marie to honor the saints and the Loas. Depending on the occasion, Marie saw God as either Jehovah or Bondye.

At 18, she married Jacques Paris who disappeared after a few years and was later discovered dead. It is said she had two children with him; however, none of them survived and passed away when they were young. After they found her husband dead, she used the term "Widow Paris" to refer herself. They also write this name on her tomb.

Her second marriage was with a French man Jean Louis Christophe Duminy de Glapion. Some say they never married. It is reported that they had 15 children in rapid succession. However, most of them died because of different diseases with yellow fever being the most prominent one as its outbreaks were common in that era in New Orleans. This eventually stopped her hairdressing profession to dedicate all of her powers to raising her family. Still, by no means, did Marie lose a client, once she plunged into home life. She also set about becoming the legendary Voodoo Queen of New Orleans.

Marie was active in social and community work. Her charity work made her a unique personality. Some of her community work includes nursing people who suffered from yellow fever and counseling condemned prisoners before they were put to death. She would also fight against execution. Since she devoted most part of her life in performing notable community service acts, it will not be wrong to state that she became a folk hero of that era.

It is believed that both Marie's mother and grandmother were voodoo practitioners. Similar to her mother, Marie had Creole, Choctaw, and Catholic creeds. Her spirituality incorporated Native American shamanism; African inspired Yoruba-based Caribbean-style Voodoo, not to mention European inspired Christianity. One thing to remember is Marie Laveau practiced Voodoo and not Hoodoo. There are many differences between these two. Voodoo is considerably more shaped by Yoruba and is devoutly followed by spiritualists worshipping more than one god or goddess, whereas Hoodoo is more influenced by Christianity and somewhat loosely practiced by spiritualists worshipping one. Those enslaved in New Orleans held many of the traditions of their West African ancestors with Voodoo. While, where the concentration of enslaved Africans was dense, in the Mississippi Delta, they followed Hoodoo beneath a much larger umbrella of darkness.

Marie worked this practice, passing on to her elder daughter, who continued practicing voodoo after Marie died in 1881.

Marie, after the death of her first husband, worked as a hairdresser to support her family. It is believed that her clients included wealthy and elite white socialites. She also had slaves who would give information regarding her clients and other notable information related to them. Marie used this information to her advantage and convinced others she had mystical powers. She used to advise the people who used to visit her on different matters of their life, i.e., relationships, legal procedures, etc. In a short period, her popularity got widespread; Marie Laveau overthrew the other voodoo queens of New Orleans. She acted as an oracle (a person who predicts the future), conducted private rituals behind her cottage on St. Ann Street in the French Quarter, performed exorcisms and offered sacrifices to spirits. Oral traditions suggested that the occult part of her magic mixed Roman Catholic beliefs, including saints; with African spirits and religious concepts. Marie Laveau received the title of New Orleans's Voodoo Queen.

Some people believe that Marie was seen around the place they buried her after the demise. It has become a popular tourist attraction in New Orleans.

It cannot be said with certainty whether she actually possessed mystical powers or she was just a clever lady who used the knowledge provided to her by clients and slaves in a courteous manner. However, it doesn't take away from the fact that her noble deeds and community work deserve respect and applause.

Priestess Miriam Chamani

Miriam Chamani, born Mary Robin Adams, is one of the most notable voodoo queens in present-day New Orleans. Brought up in Mississippi, Miriam Chamani states she has had visions and strange occurrences since childhood. Born to laborers in Pocahontas, Mississippi, Mary Robin Adams took on the role Priestess Miriam, when she began her spiritual practice.

Intensively raised Baptist in rural Mississippi during the post–World War II, she displayed an early inclination toward reverence, as her family remembers her talk to spirits as a child. Less than a week after finishing high school and avoiding the rigid Jim Crow-era South, she took off to work in New York as a housekeeper in 1962.

Following serving as a housekeeper in New York for many years, Miriam relocated to Chicago and started in a nursing curriculum in 1966. There, Miriam was given an introduction to the Spiritual Church, which fused Voodoo, Native American, and Protestant-Catholic religious influences.

Miriam met Oswan Chamani in 1989. He was a priest of Obeah, an Afro-American folk magic and faith structure from his native country of Belize. Obeah, much like Voodoo and Santeria, has origins as a method of defiance in the New World African slave cultures. Miriam and Osman shortly left for New Orleans and wed in 1990. They carried out divination readings at Marie Laveau's House of Voodoo. The couple was associated with the New Orleans Historic Voodoo Museum before founding the Voodoo Spiritual Temple.

Priestess Miriam has combined her medical education with her spiritual background, perceiving that Marie Laveau used her curative experience of herbs both in her work as

Marie nursed the sick during yellow fever outbreaks and in rendering religious ceremonies. Priestess Miriam blends her Spiritual Church training, her medical education, and the spiritual and herbal healing procedures she acquired from her husband to assist those who pay a visit to the Voodoo Spiritual Temple.

Since her husband's death in 1995, Miriam has overseen the New Orleans Voodoo Spiritual Temple and Cultural Center, where she gives readings, rituals, and other spiritual services. The Temple, situated in the French Quarter across from the entrance to Armstrong Park, concentrates on West African spiritual and herbal healing.

She holds readings and sessions at the Temple and performs rituals in the courtyard. Priestess Miriam often gives interviews with the news and entertainment media. She is currently married to Allen Villeneuve.

TEN

Voodoo Kings

Doctor John

Doctor John, also called Prince John or Bayou John, born as a part of the Bambara Tribe of Senegal, Doctor John was captured by Spanish slave traders and sent to Cuba. After being freed by a kind master, he worked as a ship's cook, before eventually relocating to Louisiana. Doctor John carried the familiarity of the craft from his home. He entered an already famous voodoo society that existed in New Orleans since the early 1700s formed by many diverse African slave groups.

Within Doctor John's work in the healing aspects of Voodoo, he earned a distinction for being an exceptional healer. Some stories went as far to declare that he had the capacity able to revive patients on the brink of death with his rituals. Many say this is one of the earliest accounts of Voodoo reanimation, beginning to the legend of zombies in Louisiana.

He started telling fortunes. Doctor John was skilled at reading people. Soon he had plenty of money saved to purchase a house. At the top of his popularity, Doctor John was estimated to be worth more than $50,000. That would be close to one million dollars today.

John maintained a harem of close to fifteen wives which he insisted on having married according to African customs. Most of those women were purchased as slaves, and they had several children with him. At one point he coupled with Voodoo Queen Marie Laveau to sell spells, potions, and charms.

He was cheated numerous times by shady businessmen that stole away his wealth. He ended up broke, destitute and living with one of his daughters.

Frank Staten aka Prince aka Papa Midnight

Born in Haiti in 1937, Frank Staten was a New Orleans nightclub performer generally identified as the Chicken Man. with his family, Staten, moved to New Orleans as a baby, where he was reared by his grandparents, who were also of Haitian descent. Frank's grandparents told him that he was of aristocratic African lineage when he was young and had supernatural capacities. From that time forward, Frank was no longer called by his given alias. His proper name was disclosed to him, and Frank would be acknowledged as Prince Ke'eyama. Having his grandmother taught him about the magic power of herbs, Prince also learned the ancient mysteries of Haitian Voodoo that had started in their native slave country of Africa and how to use them to help others. With the firm guidance of his grandparents, Prince became more powerful every day. He started to adhere to a rigid diet that he believed was revealed to him through prayer and meditation. Prince mentioned he was shown that the typical chicken was his most potent course. As directed, Prince made chicken a part of his everyday diet. Adhering to the strictures revealed to him, Prince soon learned that he could control every aspect of his physical body.

Not only would he eat chicken every day, but Prince found he could chew and swallow glass without getting harmed, and that he could actually eat fire. Papa John Bayou showed Prince the ways of Haitian Voodoo.

Prince made numerous trips to voodoo communities, as a young man, in Haiti and the United States to study more of the craft.

Prince became Papa Midnight and lived permanently in New Orleans in the 1970s. With his established Chicken Man persona, he exhibited his deep spiritual relationship with Voodoo and God. His show consisted of magic, dancing, and biting the head off a live chicken and consuming its blood. He drew thousands of fans, but some Voodoo practitioners viewed him purely as a showman. Frank Staten was worshipped as a Voodoo priest until his inexplicable death in early 1998. His ashes were presented to the Voodoo Spiritual Temple.

ELEVEN

Voodoo Practices: What You Need To Know

The word voodoo is sure to send chills down your spine as it evokes the art of black magic, bewitching, zombies, spiritual control from the realm beyond the physical, and graveyard magic through go-betweens that control the said person using dolls in which the spirit of the person now is invoked into.

The word also is also associated with pins pricking dolls, candles, incense burning, and blood sacrifices from chicken, goat or cows while the priest dances in all white incanting unrecognizable words and blowing white powder to conjure the spirits of the living and the dead.

However, all these are the creative imagery of what voodoo is not what voodoo is all about. Yes, this is not the real picture of what voodoo originally is, but of other people practicing dark magic with voodoo.

The voodoo we know and see is what the movies and people with sinister motives have turned it out to be. So with that said, what is voodoo?

Since voodoo is a religion of experiences, pains, sufferings, and responsibilities, it wasn't difficult to hand down the beliefs to the next generations.

Voodoo Candles

Candle-burning is an essential part of many religions and rituals around the globe.

The candle is the light which the living (person burning the candle) uses to connect with the spirits or God uttering specific chants, prayers or performing an action for a particular purpose or to achieve an aim or get answers to prayer.

Using candles is known to bring Good Luck, Money, Love, Wealth, Health, Protection, etc. The candles also come in different colors symbolizing different reasons and intentions. When using a voodoo candle for any purpose, the candles are rubbed with anointing oils or oil for the purpose it is to be used for.

How to Use the Voodoo Candle?

For whatever reason you want to use the candle, the first thing is to carve the name of the person on the candle before burning it, for example, if you seek the truth from a friend or someone that hurt you. You do the following:

Dress the candle with the name of the person you want the truth from

Rub the candle down with the anointing oil specifically for the purpose

Lit the candle and speak the word repeating the person's name over and over.

The candle is also used to keep a loved one, make money, pay a debt, and whatever you want.

Types of Colored Candles and Their Meanings

Brown Candles – for restoration or wins a legal battle

Black Candles – to send back evil forces

White Candles – for spiritual healing and purity

Blue Candles – bring good intentions, joy, and unity

Green Candles – wealth, getting rich, a bountiful harvest or a good job

Red Candles – love, passion and good health

Yellow Candles – attraction, friendship and answered prayers

Pink Candles - Romance and good attraction
White and Black Candles – to return evil arrow to their senders
Green and Black Candles – to break any jinx over money and not making it
Red and Black Candles – to break a love spell
Orange Candle – when changing plans or seeking to know the future
Purple Candle – power and ambition

Voodoo Oils

The oils are just like the candles and are mostly used together to get the power of the spirits working and faster. The oils are meant to ease the journey of the spirit through the land of the spirits to the physical.

They serve different purposes, but homemade oils are more effective and potent than other oils. The homemade oils are made with the purest essential oils and sacred herbs found from the locality and the purpose.

Uses of Voodoo Oils

Some oils are worn as a scent to attract good luck and prosperity.

They are used to gain power and influence of another person by rubbing it on them

They are used to dress a candle before a candle ritual

They are used to bath and on the skin for spiritual cleansing

They can be used to draw love or attract a particular love interest

They can be used to influence or bend the views of another

They are placed in workplaces with other material to get good luck in your workspace and protect you against the evil eye

Types of Voodoo Oil

Some very common oils are:

The Four Thieves Oil
For Protection against Calamities and Ailments
20 drops Clove Essential Oil
15 drops Lemon Essential Oil
10 drops Cinnamon Essential Oil
10 drops Eucalyptus Essential Oil
5 drops Rosemary Essential Oil

To purify a house or yourself from negativity. Use as a floor wash with black salt in house cleansing rituals. Use in your bath for cleansing one's self.

The Uncrossing Oil
To Shake Off Spells, Jinxes, Black Magic and Plain Old Bad Luck From Yourself
Poke root
Rue
Sandalwood
Use Sunflower Oil as the base.

Set all ingredients into a bottle or jar and let to sit in the sun for a month. To use, anoint your body by tracing the symbol of the cross above your brow, heart, hands, and feet in this order. If it's the crossing of an individual's sexual energy, or the root of the condition was an ex-partner, anoint the privates also. Do this before marking your feet. Lastly, mark the back of your neck. You will walk away (or the person you are working this for) without glancing back till you reach an outlying spot, such as your property line, crossroads, etc. petition for God to remove your troubles. You will of even the most unshakable misfortunes, be released.

Come To Me Oil
Romance and Love
5 drops Patchouli Essential Oil
1 drop Ginger Essential Oil
6 drops Rose Essential Oil
A Pinch Dried Patchouli,
A Pinch Dried Ginger Root

A Pinch Dried Rose Petals

I find Grapeseed carrier oil works best.

Use with gris-gris, candles, etc. to win the attention and affection of someone who interests you.

Obey My Command Oil

1 teaspoon Calamus Root

1 teaspoon Licorice Root

Almond Oil base

Tag lock from your intended such as hair, name on paper, blood, and picture, nail clippings, etc.

Allow mixture to sit outside from full moon to full moon.

Wearing oil to help you command the person or situation you intend.

Abundance Oil

To Draw Wealth and Prosperity

4 Drops Vanilla

1 Drop Vetivert

Can be utilized in a ritual or spell intended at increasing your wealth and prosperity. Use this oil for success with money, business, love, family, companionship, freedom from debt, etc.

Road Opener

To Hasten a Breakthrough

10 drops Lemon

10 drops Orange

Bits of Dried Lemon Peel

Bits of Dried Orange Peel

2 drops Orange Food Color

Small Skeleton Key

Use with gris-gris, dolls, etc. to clear away obstacles and open roads for new opportunities. Clear the path in life so you can push ahead.

How to Use Voodoo Oil

Any oils you pick involves specific steps and strict ways of using them. Using commanding oil as an example:

The Commanding Oil is to gain the upper hand over someone either as a love interest or to get the final say during business deals. It's been said that the oil can completely overcome the free will of the other person.

To use the oil; anoint the right candle that suits your intention and says the incantations. Afterward, rub the oil on the picture or on an object to be placed where the person will pass, step or stop or even with a handshake.

This will ensure they keep their promise and never break the agreement with you.

BONUS! Creating Your Oils

Making your oils is not that tough. It's really straightforward. First, figure out your intent. Whether you're making a protection oil for home and family, money oil to draw prosperity to you, it's all about the purpose.

Once you've determined your intent, collect the essential oils called for in the recipe. In a clean jar or bowl, add 1/8 Cup of base oil. You can use:

Almond Oil
Grapeseed Oil (my favorite!)
Jojoba Oil
Olive Oil
Safflower Oil
Sunflower Oil

To begin, if you are blending an oil to anoint your body, be sure you're not adding any components that are irritating to the skin.

Using an eyedropper, add the essential oils from the recipe to your desired oil base. Be sure to observe the suggested ratios. To mix, you need to swirl the blend, don't stir it. Swirl the oils into the base oil using a clockwise direction.

Store your oils in dark-colored glass bottles. Make sure you stock your oil mixtures in a spot away from heat and moisture. Label them with their name and write the date on the label. In a dark bottle, all your mixtures will look the same. You want to use inside six months.

Voodoo Spirit Dolls

Voodoo spirit dolls are the most commonly used object in to conjure the spirit of a person into a doll to do as you say. The dolls are created from corn husks, potatoes, tree parts or stuffed cloth.

The dolls are meant to address a person's spirit, and with the power of the gods, your pleas, prayers, and desires are answered.

How Does It Work?

To communicate with a person spirit; a colored pin and charm stuck on the doll that is a replica of the person you are trying to contact or use. Remember that the doll must contain a piece of the person like a piece of cloth, nail or hair attached to the doll.

Using an object from the person allow you to speak directly to the right spirit during the ritual process. You can talk directly to the spirit of the person through the doll, instruct, send on a mission, beg for forgiveness, question it, and persuade it to carry out a job or destroy it.

The voodoo doll is not used for all bad though; it can be used as an object to praying for a person spirit, health, job, career, marriage or for good luck. To invoke the powers of the spirit, you will need candles, oils, and drums to summon the spirit and send a more explicit message.

Types of Voodoo Dolls

There are different types of voodoo dolls for all purposes ranging from healing, money, wealth, revenge, guidance, protection, laying curses and fertility. Each doll has a different color that means different things. For example;

Black Dolls - used to send away negative energy or invoke one to destroy someone life.

Blue Dolls – for peace, love, and tranquility.

Yellow Dolls – to increase success and confidence.

Purple Dolls – to communicate with the spirit realm, draw wisdom from the spirits or explore the psychic world.

Green Dolls - for an increase in business, at work or for fertility.

White Dolls – goodness, purity, healing, and positivity.

Red Dolls – for love, to attract a love interest and power.

It is clear now that voodoo dolls are not initially for evil even though that is what is depicted in movies and used by dubious and evil people. So it is a mistake to believe that voodoo dolls are for bad, harm or vengeance instead of good.

Mojo Bags

Mojo bags are little bags that hold magical items made by a voodoo priest or priestess to protect the user from evil and to also grant them their heart desires.

These bags are created to the specification of the owners and what they want. They are said to possess magical and physical powers and prayers for the person in question.

The finished bags are pinned in the inner clothing like a bra, the underside of your cloth and are for great purposes to the wearer.

How Does The Mojo Bag Work?

The person that needs help come to the voodooist, and states their request. The mojo bag is created according to what you want. A mojo bag that does one or two tasks is more effective than one that is made to perform a range of work.

The initial step in constructing your mojo bag is to choose a cloth bag whose color resonates with your objective. Once again, here is a list to help you determine the most appropriate color for your mojo bag.

Black – Freedom from evil. Transformation.

Blue – Peace, tranquility, psychic ability, loyalty, Blue justice, truth, meditation, astral travel, kindness, wisdom, depresses excess energy, relieves worry and stress, and helps insomnia.

Brown – Stability, fertility, thrift, work, control, Brown conquering, success in business, concentration, grounding, long term achievements, growth, determination, planting.

Green – Fertility, money, employment, better business Green is creative ideas, rewards, good luck. Green is Earth, plants, growing.

Gray – Neutralizes stress, negativity, lessens the impact of mistakes. Gray signifies Silver. As a blend of white and black, it is used to remove negativity, cleanse undesired energies, break a spell of poor luck, and exorcisms. Silver gray can help to figure out and work with Karma and previous life recall.

Orange – Can also be accepted for Gold, indicates success, mental clarity, discipline, tranquility, joyfulness, brings luck and money and adds happiness and flexibility. Helps break out of the slump or a rut. Connected with the Sun and Mars. For healing, provides necessary energy, peace of mind, determination.

Pink – Spiritual love, romance, prosperity, attraction, Pink conquers hate and evil, draws compassion, understanding, kindness, friendship, overcomes anger, brings forgiveness for others, from others, from self. Helps heal the hurts of abuse, accidents or injury, allows for self love and self-respect. Heals broken hearts conquers discord.

Purple – A combination of the Blue and Red Energy. Purple can overcome odds or competition, to attain work success, control, respect, wealth, dignity, honor, obedience, command, court cases, concentration, victory, repels negativity.

Red – Power, passion, protection, energy, enthusiasm. Red conquers fear, strength in battle, associated with the West, the planet Mars and Tuesday's Element – Fire. Heals anemia or when there has been blood loss builds strength and power for those weakened by fatigue.

Silver – Gray often used for Silver. Quick money, gambling, moon magick.

Yellow – Attraction, success, drawing, communicating, for studying, memory, clear thinking, decision making, charm, burnt for those who have passed away. In healing for successful treatment, clears away depression, draws happiness, confidence.

White – All-purpose spiritual awareness and power. Purity, truth, religious devotion, cooperation, assistance.

Once you have decided the appropriate bag, you must empower it. Begin by scoring a candle with your intention. Impale the candle with nine pins, affirming your desire with the insertion of each pin. The ninth and final pin should be stuck straight through the wick of the candle. Burn some incense and then light your candle.

Ingredients of a Mojo Bag

What you place in your mojo bag is as, if not more, significant than the bag's color. Load the bag with the matching herbs, crystals, stones, and symbols of your objective.

Sample Herbs for Love

Adam and Eve Root - Primarily used by lovers where one lover keeps the Eve Root, and the other lover keeps the Adam Root. It's said that it keeps your lover faithful to you and hinders rivals. You can also carry both roots in a small bag all the time to draw a love toward you, or for a marriage offer.

Balm of Gilead Tears - For love, protection, and help in healing from the loss of a loved one.

Coriander - Love, protection, and health. Add to love spells and charms to draw romance or use in a ritual activity to reduce the pain of a broken love affair.

Passion Flower - Stimulates emotional stability, peace, attracts friendship and prosperity. Increases the sexual drive, as it is used in love spells.

Ylang Ylang - To increase sexual attraction and influence.

Sample Herbs for Money

Allspice - Money, luck, obtaining abundance and healing. Produces added power and strength to any spells and charms.

Cinnamon - For success, healing, psychic powers, protection, spirituality, passion, love.

Cloves - Magical uses include protection, exorcism, love, money, and good luck. Cleanses the aura.

High John - Useful in all ritual work associated with prosperity.

Nutmeg - Carry nutmeg for good luck, and to increase psychic powers. Use in money and prosperity spells.

Once you have added all of the relevant items to your mojo bag, pull the drawstring closed securely and tie the strings into a knot, keeping the bag shut. Fasten the two ends into a second knot, wrapping the ends underneath themselves. Recite these words as you tie your bag:

"With these knots, I bind you to this purpose."

Once you have secured your bag, you must "feed' it by blessing it with similar oil. As you sprinkle or rub the oil on the bag, say "With this oil, I give you the power to carry out your purpose."

Over time, your mojo bag may require to be replenished. This is generally accomplished near the fall equinox, in late September. This process involves taking the mojo bag apart, keeping the hard items and taking out and replacing leafy/dried herbs. The contents are then reconstructed into a new mojo bag, which is prayed over and fed. Some individuals believe that a mojo's power generally lasts for a year, and should be buried after that time. Others think that if your mojo bag is still working for you do not perform any changes.

Your mojo bag is for your eyes and hands only. Do not let anyone else touch or see it. You can talk to it and ask for its direct help at any time. This potent manifestation tool will allow you in an infinite of ways to quickly and effortlessly obtain your wishes.

Remember, when the mojo bag is made, a prayer is spoken

over the bag, and the bag is fed to activate it. Furthermore, depending on the mojo bag you are carrying, you must place the mojo bag in the right spot to work well. For Example:

A Kiss Me mojo bag is carried in your pockets near your private to attract sexual attention from the opposite sex. For wealth and money, keep a mojo bag in your wallet. Hide a Stay With Me mojo bag in your partner's wardrobe or underwear drawer to keep them home. Place a mojo bag at the entrance of a home for peace.

The Gris-Gris Bag

This is like the mojo bag but made explicitly to ward off an evil spirit and have their roots deep in Africa and Islam.

A typical gris-gris bag will contain Arabic writings, different objects like a coin, feather, flannel, stones, herbs and even sand from a graveyard to attract the jinni (spirit) that will protect you from evil.

The bag is used by believer and non-believers and can be seen attached to buildings, in office, cars, and home. Most times they are not kept in the open except as instructed by the maker.

However, as time pass, the gris-gris fell into the hands of people that were not Muslim but believed in magic hence used magical inscriptions to replace the Arabic writings.

There are the five elements to remember when creating a gris-gris bag.

Color symbolism is essential. Choose a color specific to your need.

It must include an odd number of items. Never an even number. It should be more than three, but never more than 13.

Fill your gris-gris with things that are specific to the desired purpose.

Dress it with a liquid of some kind.

Finally, smudge the gris-gris with incense or candle. Or, you can breathe on it.

To use a gris-gris bag, take it and concentrate on the desire or need that you have. Imagine yourself achieving your goal by forming a clear vision of yourself obtaining what it is you desire in your mind. Do this exercise as often as possible. Set your gris-gris bag in a specific place to remind you of your desire or need. Women typically carry them in their bras or on the left side, while men carry them on the right side.

Herbs and Resins That Can Be Used

Black Salt - Absorb and trap negative energies. Eliminate bad neighbors.

Catnip - For love, beauty, happiness and cat magic.

Chamomile - Used for meditation, relaxation, sleep, and drawing love and money.

Coltsfoot - Used to achieve psychic visions, add to love sachets, also for spells involving serenity.

Copal Tears Resin - For love, and divination and purification

Frankincense - Burn as an offering to Gods, to expel evil spirits, divination, meditation.

Jasmine - For love and wealth, Add to sachets. For prophetic dreams, Burn in the bedroom.

Lavender - To enhance happiness. Used in love spells and purification rituals.

Mandrake - To ensure house protection and prosperity, hang over your doorway. Carry a piece with you for protection.

Mistletoe - Not just for kisses! Hang above the doorway or the bed for protection from nightmares and evil spirits.

Mugwort - Used for dreams, divination, intuition, protection, and psychic powers.

Myrrh - Meditation, peace, purification and hex breaking

Penny Royal - Use as a traveler's protection, peace, and removes curses.

Rose Buds - A common ingredient in love spells. Rosebuds are also used for prophetic dreams and relaxation.

Saltpeter - Reduce male sex drive, expedites up money spells

Skull Cap - Used for attraction and money spells. Also supports faithfulness in relationships,

Spearmint - Burn to attract your lover. To protect children, hang in a sachet in the bedroom.

Valerian - Use for sleep, love, purification, protection, and serenity.

Vervain - For love, protection, peace

Fortune Telling the Future

The power to know what the future holds belongs to God alone, but God also has gifted people this power to see into the unknown. Although not all of them are true, the idea of wanting to know our future and what it holds has been a passion and dying desire since the beginning of time.

How Do They Do It?

How fortune tellers do it has no scientific backings yet, and it has defile human imagination, but whether you give credence to it or not, there are people with the ability to tell the future. Fortune tellers are known to read stars (like the three wise men in the bible), or other methods like tarot card, divination, or your spirit.

It honestly doesn't matter how many times they hit gold, but seeing a fortune teller is for fun and should surely not be something to lose sleep about.

Finally, magic, voodoo, mojo bags or fortune telling are things that only come to pass when we allow our imagination to dance on the dark side of our thoughts. We are not disputing the power of darkness and what they are capable of, but we have an even bigger power to deflect the darkness in our lives and seek divine consultation from God alone.

TWELVE

Voodoo Symbols

Veves

In the Voodoo practice, a veve is an elaborate symbol of a Loa and is applied in invocation rituals. It serves as their representation during ceremonies. Each Loa possesses his or her individual veve, which are painted permanently on the walls of the hounfort, or is outlined on the ground with maveve, finely powdered eggshell, wheat flour, red brick powder, bark, gunpowder, chalk, charcoal, ashes or material of a similar appearance, before a ritual. Sacrifices and offerings are usually placed upon them.

A veve is thought to be more potent if it is rendered with precise details. The more mindful attention given to the accuracies of the particulars, the higher its ability to invoke the Loa successfully. Such a design symbolizes a Loa to be invoked. Acting as a magnet, it obliging the spirit which it represents to descend to earth and appear at the ritual. Veves delivers both as a focal position for invocation as well as a form of an altar for offerings.

The designs incorporate well-recognized traditional elements but also reflect the individual intentions and creative skill of the male priest, known as a Houngan or female priestess who would be a Mambo.

Despite the elaborate care and skill with which they are drawn, the Veves are generally destroyed by the end of the ceremony, blown away or swept apart by dancing feet.

Here are Veves for a few Loas mentioned earlier.

Ayizan

Voodoo of Louisiana

Baron Samedi

Damballah

Simbi

Marassa

Voodoo of Louisiana

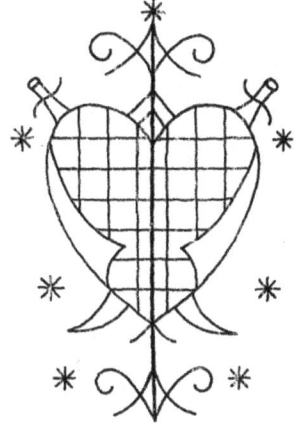

Erzulie Dantor

Erzulie Freda

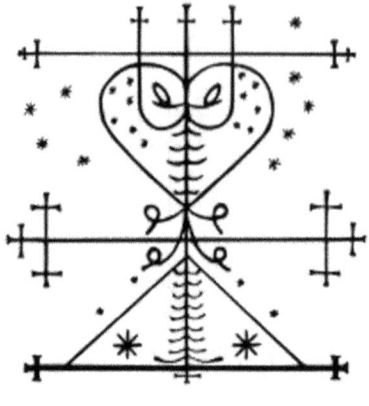

Maman Brigitte

Ogoun

Voodoo of Louisiana

Papa Legba

Glossary

Agassou: The all-important Dahomean Leopard. The Spiritual belief of removal.
Agouer: The Spiritual beliefs of natural order and abundance.
Aïda: The Spiritual principle of exponential gradation.
Ainsi Soit-il: So mote it be. Amen. Thus it is.
Aïsan or Aïzan: The Spiritual source of evolution.
Algiers Point: Where slaves were sold.
Ancestors: Those who have gone before.
Ancient Egypt: A source of Voodoo along with Nubia.
Bayou St John: Winding from Lake Pontchartrain, the bayou where special Voodoo rituals in times past were practiced.
Black Eagles: The Mardi Gras Indians.
Boko: A Voodoo priest who uses black magic. A Boko is different from an Oungan or Mambo.
Bondye: The Supreme Being recognized as God. Obtained from the French Bon Dieu, meaning "good God."
Bonne Chance: Good Luck.
Bossu: The spiritual principle of controlled expansion.

Glossary

Boussilage: A buildup of moss and mud. Similar to adobe bricks.

Brigitte: the spiritual principle of containment.

Catholic Church: Similar to Voodoo as they have saints, we have saints, etc.

Cercueil: Coffin.

Chicken Man: His ashes abide in Priestess Miriam Chamani's Voodoo Spiritual Temple.

Chifforobe: Place for a hidden altar.

Confondre: To confuse

Connaitre l'Loa: To meet a Loa.

Corbeau: A crow.

Creoles: A native resident of New Orleans. Initial settlers in the New World including their descendants, both African and European. Future generations of these colonists and slaves.

Croisailler: To crisscross or overlap.

Cross: To put a spell on someone or to interfere with someone's activities.

Crossroads: A place where two roads, two worlds intersect.

Cypress Trees: Swamp trees.

Doctor John: A well-known Root Doctor in New Orleans. Born John Montenet.

Eau: Water.

Entortiller: To entangle or twist.

Envoyer: To send.

Fait Accompli: The spell is done.

Gagner: To win, to have, to obtain.

Gifts: We do not sacrifice for our Loas, no give sacrifices to them. We give them presents.

Graveyard: Where certain spells are executed.

Gris-Gris: In New Orleans voodoo, one of the most spellbinding charm, which blends black and white magic.

Guinée: The Motherland, Africa.

Glossary

Haiti: Another center for Voodoo.
Helping Hand: Spiritual support for those in crisis.
Hoodoo: An African-American belief of folk magic, herbal medicine, and conjuring; not connected to Voodoo.
Hounfort: A voodoo temple.
Houngan: A Voodoo Priest.
Hounsi: A Voodoo initiate.
Incantation: A chant executed while casting a spell.
Juju: In New Orleans Voodoo, a charm mainly used in positive, or healing, magic.
Kalfou: The intersections where good and evil converge; the sacred area where offerings are conducted.
Loa or Lwa: The supernatural, eternal spirits who oversee various areas of the physical world and human existence. Related to saints, individuals can petition them for help.
Lougarou: A black magician who can transform into an animal. A vampire who drinks blood from kids.
Mambo: A fully initiated priestess of Voodoo.
Marie Laveau: The most well-known New Orleans Voodoo Queen.
Mojo: A charm that brings to its holder a precise, well-defined compensation, such as money, passion or protection in New Orleans Voodoo.
New Orleans Witchcraft: Practical witchcraft. Used to obtain those things which you desire.
Ouanga: A malevolent charm used by a Boko in black magic. Also spelled wanga.
Ouangateur: An individual who crosses another individual with a charm.
Oungan: A fully initiated priest of Voodoo.
Papa Legba: The most potent Loa. He guards the gateway between the material and spiritual realms. Those wanting to contact with other Loa first must honor him through ritual and gifts.

Glossary

Peristyle: The public space of a Voodoo Temple where public ritual practices take place.

Point: The focus of power and magical force.

Racine: Root

Revenant: A ghost or spook.

Salive: Saliva.

Saint or Sainte: A Loa

Sanite Dede: Voodoo Queen before Marie Laveau.

Voodooist: A practitioner of Voodoo.

Zombi: A body without a soul that a Boko has raised up from the dead to use as slave labor.

About the Author

Monique Joiner Siedlak is a writer, witch, and warrior on a mission to awaken people to their greatest potential through the power of storytelling infused with mysticism, modern paganism, and new age spirituality. At the young age of 12, she began rigorously studying the fascinating philosophy of Wicca. By the time she was 20, she was self-initiated into the craft, and hasn't looked back ever since. To this day, she has authored over 40 books pertaining to the magick and mysteries of life.

To find out more about Monique Joiner Siedlak artistically, spiritually, and personally, feel free to visit her **official website**.

www.mojosiedlak.com

facebook.com/mojosiedlak
twitter.com/mojosiedlak
instagram.com/mojosiedlak
pinterest.com/mojosiedlak
bookbub.com/authors/monique-joiner-siedlak

Other Books by Monique Joiner Siedlak

Practical Magick

Wiccan Basics

Candle Magick

Wiccan Spells

Love Spells

Abundance Spells

Herb Magick

Moon Magick

Creating Your Own Spells

Gypsy Magic

Personal Growth and Development

Creative Visualization

Astral Projection for Beginners

Meditation for Beginners

Reiki for Beginners

Manifesting With the Law of Attraction

Stress Management

The Yoga Collective

Yoga for Beginners

Yoga for Stress

Yoga for Back Pain

Yoga for Weight Loss

Yoga for Flexibility

Yoga for Advanced Beginners

Yoga for Fitness

Yoga for Runners

Yoga for Energy

Yoga for Your Sex Life

Yoga: To Beat Depression and Anxiety

Yoga for Menstruation

A Natural Beautiful You

Creating Your Own Body Butter

Creating Your Own Body Scrub

Creating Your Own Body Spray

THANK YOU FOR READING MY BOOK! I REALLY APPRECIATE ALL OF YOUR FEEDBACK AND I LOVE TO HEAR WHAT YOU HAVE TO SAY. PLEASE LEAVE YOUR REVIEW AT YOUR FAVORITE RETAILER!